THE STRAIGHTFORWARD

BEGINNER'S GUIDE TO LEARNING

PYTHON PROGRAMMING.

Contents

3

4

Introduction to Python

Popular high-level, all-purpose programming language Python. It was developed by the Python foundation after being created by Guido van Possum in 1991. Because of programming's syntax, which was developed with code readability in mind, programmers may be able to express their thoughts in less code.

Programming language called Python makes it possible to work quickly and integrate systems more successfully.

The most widely used Python versions are Python 2 and Python 3. Both are very different.
Twitter is a dynamic, byte code-compiled, and interpreted language.

Variable, parameter, function, and method types are not declared in the source code. You sacrifice the source code's compile-time type verification but get short, flexible code as a result.

Describe Python.

Guido van Possum developed the all-purpose programming language Python in the 1980s. It is the most well-liked programming language globally in 2023 because it is so flexible, adaptable, and user-friendly for beginners.

The most widely used and simplest to learn programming language is Python. It offers a strong community and experienced resources accessible in addition to a large pool of employment opportunities across all sectors and vocations. According to the PYPL and TIOBE ranking, Python defeated C to become the top programming language in June 2023.

- Python is designed for a wide variety of applications rather than for the solution of particular issues, such as:

- Automation Data Science Web Development Software Development Analytics

It's Simple to Use and Teach Python

Due to its ease of use and comprehension, Python is a suitable choice for beginners. The language boasts the most straightforward syntax of any programming language in use today, making it the most accessible. It also prioritizes natural language above any other programming language. Python's ease of use and understanding allow for much faster creation and execution of routines than with other programming languages. Python's popularity has grown dramatically in part due to the simplicity with which programmers of all skill levels can comprehend and produce its code.

Use of Python in Web Development

Python is allegedly one of the most useful programming languages, according to experts in web development. The availability of its many different applications with ready-made solutions to basic web development tasks increases the speed of a single project.

Programming Language Versatile

Python is renowned for its adaptability, which enables you to use it for a variety of jobs. Let's explore Python's use cases in more detail.

Machine Learning and Data Visualization

Python may be used to visualize data as pie charts, histograms, and bar and line graphs. Additionally, you may handle data science more effectively and efficiently by using Python frameworks like Tensor Flow.

Analytical Statistics

Python makes it easier to carry out difficult statistical computations, saving you time and effort when manipulating and evaluating them.

Language is Frequently Used in Data Science

Whatever route you choose, data is going to remain important to the IT sector. Python is presently widely used in data science. Experts handling modern technologies for analytics of data need to be conversant with coding languages like Python since the quantity of data generated by these tools is growing every day. To take advantage of the newest cutting-edge technology, data professionals must also remain up to date on industry developments.

A wide range of buildings and libraries

Python is especially well-liked because it provides developers with access to tens of different modules and frameworks. since of these libraries and frameworks, the language is more helpful since less time is needed. The NumPy, SciPy, Django, an and other libraries that are used for a variety of applications are some of the most well-known Python libraries.

Automation of tasks and scripting

Python is particularly helpful when you want to increase productivity by automating or scripting repetitive operations. You can expedite a number of things with Python, including

- Detecting errors
- convert files
- emails being sent
- internet content discovery
- Elimination of redundant data
- rudimentary math calculation

ML tools could make use of Python.

Python is utilized for big data and machine learning research to advance these domains. Python is very useful in the AI business and is also utilized in data science, robotics, and other areas of technological growth.

Python in Education

In college and university courses, the emphasis on the language is growing. Python is so often used in fields like data science, artificial intelligence, deep learning, and others, which explains why. Additionally, it is crucial that schools and businesses include the language into their curricula given the sizable number of students interested in pursuing jobs in technology.

Routine Tasks

Python might also help non-programmers like social media administrators and journalists by simplifying their regular tasks. Python may be used to automatically update procurement lists, move data from text files to spreadsheets, and track stock market values, among other things.

Compatible with the Iota the Internet of Things (Iota) is a large network of interconnected gadgets and technology that enables device and cloud communication. Famous Iota instances include:

The Smart Home

Activity trackers for connected vehicles
Wearable technology with augmented reality.

Has a very charitable community

One of the longest and most popular programming languages is since. As a result, it had the chance to create a vibrant community of developers, and coders. Students studying Python will benefit from having the support they need to easily learn the skills required by industry and get the right training.

Continuity and flexibility

Python is a flexible language that provides programmers plenty of room to experiment with new ideas. Python experts won't simply remain with the status quo; they'll try to develop new processes, technology, or applications. Developers may concentrate on learning only one tongue and use their skills to the fullest extent since it provides them the independence and flexibility they need.

Installation and Setup Guide for Python 3

Putting Python into Windows

On Windows, there are five installation techniques:

Google Play Store

The complete Linux installation for Windows Subsystem

You'll discover how to verify whether Python is installed on your Windows machine in this section. Additionally, you'll discover which of the three installation techniques you need to choose. Check out Your Jingo Coding Environment on Windows: Setup tutorial for a more detailed setup tutorial.

How to Determine the Python Version on Windows

To see whether Danto is already installed on your Windows PC, use a command-line software like PowerShell.

As a suggestion, here's how to start PowerShell:

Press Win, and then type PowerShell to get started.
Put the key in.
By right-clicking the Start button, you may choose either Windows PowerShell with Azure PowerShell (Admin).
You may also use Windows Terminal or cmd.exe.

Note: Refer to Using the Terminal on Windows for additional

information on your choices for the Windows terminal.

Open the command line, then type and hit Enter the following command:

the command "python --version Python 3.8.4"
You may see the installed version by using the --version switch. As an alternative, you might use the -V switch:

Python -V 3.8.4 may be found at C:
In any case, you should update your installation if you notice a version lower than 3.8.4, which was the most current version at the time of writing.

Both of the aforementioned instructions will start the Microsoft Store and take you to the Python application page if you don't already have a version of Python installed on your machine. The following part will show you how to finish the installation from the Microsoft Store.

You may use the where.exe command in PowerShell or cmd.exe to find the installation's location if you're curious:

What is syntax in Python?

The principles that are utilized to construct sentences in Python programming are all defined by the Python syntax.

For instance, in order to understand the English language, we must study grammar. In a similar vein, in order to master the Python language, you must first study and comprehend its grammar.

A syntax example in Python

Python's clean grammatical structure contributes to its popularity.

You may gain a sense of what Python programming looks like by taking a brief look at a simple Python application.

Checking if a person is eligible to vote using a simple Python program.

print("Enter your name:") after obtaining the user's name.

retrieving the user's age print("Enter your age:") name = input()

age equals int(input())

If (age >= 18), determine if the user is eligible or not:

   print(name, "is eligible to cast a ballot."

Alternatively: print(name, 'is not eligible to vote.')

Python Data Structures

Data structures are a way to organize data so that it may be accessed more rapidly depending on the situation. The fundamental building block of every programming language and the foundation of each Lists

Program is the data structure. Python is simpler to learn than other programming languages when it comes to understanding the principles of these data structures.

Lists in Python are just like arrays in other languages, which are collections of data presented in an ordered manner. A list is very flexible since its components don't have to be of the same type. Lists in Python are similar to vectors in C++ or array lists in Java. The most costly action is to add or remove a member from the List's beginning since all the components must be moved. The cost of deletion or insertion at the end of the list might increase if the reallocated RAM is all used up.

Making a Python List as an illustration

List = print(List) [1, 2, 3, "GFG", 2.3].

Tuple

A Python tuple is an accumulation of Python objects, similar to a list, except tuples are immutable by nature, meaning that once they are generated, their components cannot be changed or added to. A Tuple may have components of several kinds, much like a List.

Using a 'comma' to divide a series of values, or with or without the use of parenthesis to arrange the data sequence, creates a tuple in Python.

The creation of tuples from a single element is also possible, although it is more difficult. One element in the parentheses is insufficient; a following 'comma' is required to convert it into a tuple.

Python Tuple Operations, as an example.

Strings are used to create a Tuple.
Tuple = ('Geeks', 'For') print("Using a String in a Tuple:")
print(Tuple)

List1 = [1, 2, 4, 5, 6] print("Tuple using List: ") creates a tuple using a list.
Tuple equals tuple(list1).

# Using indexing to access an element print ("First element of tuple")
print(Tuple[0])

Accessing the final element in a tuple by using negative indexing print("Last element of tuple")
print(Tuple[-1])

```
print       ("Tuple's       third-to-last
element")
print (Tuple[-3])
```

Python String Arrays of bytes that represent Unicode characters make up strings. A string may be thought of as an immutable collection of characters. A single character in Python is just a string of length 1, as there is no such thing as a character data type.

Because strings cannot be changed, doing so will result in a new string being created.

Types of Python Operators the Python programming language supports the following types of operators.

Comparison (Relational) Operators for Arithmetic
Operators of assignments
Intelligent Operators
Operators in bits
Owners of memberships
Individual Operators
Let's quickly review each of these operators in turn.

Arithmetic Operators in Python

Mathematical operations on numerical quantities are carried out using Python's arithmetic operators. Addition, subtraction, multiplication, division, modulus, exposures, and floor division are among these operations.

Example Operator Name + Addition Subtracting 10 from 20 to get 30Multiplication: 20 - 10 = 10Division of 10 * 20 = 20020 / 10 = 2 %Floor Division Modulus 22% 10 = 2 Exponent 4**2 = 169//2 = 4

Comparison Operators in Python

The values on each side of a comparison operator in Python are compared to determine their relationship. Relational operators is another name for them. Equal, Not Equal, Greater Than, Less Than, Greater Than or Equal To, and Less Than or Equal To are these operators.

Operator Name Example!= Not Equal 4!= 5 is true. == Equal 4 == 5 is not true. Not true: Greater Than 4 > 5.

Less than 4 of 5 are true. It is not true that 4 >= 5 or greater than or equal to 4.

If 4 is less than or equal to 5, then 5.

Assignment Operators in Python

Variables may have values assigned to them using Python assignment operators. These operators contain basic assignment operators as well as operators for addition, subtraction, multiplication, division, and assign.

Example of an Operator Name is Assignment. Assignment a += 5 (Same as a = a + 5) Operator a = 10 +

Assignment for Subtraction: a -= 5 (Same as a = a - 5)

Assignment for Multiplication: a *= 5 (Same as a = a * 5)

Division Assignment: a = a/5 (also known as a = a/5)

Assignment %= Remainder a%= 5 (Equal to a = a%)

Exponent Assignment a = 2 (also known as a = a ** 2)

Floor Division Assignment an is equal to 3 (also known as a = a // 3)

Bitwise operators in Python

Bitwise operators operate bit by bit and operate on bits. Consider the case where a = 60 and b = 13. In this case, their values in binary form would be 0011 1100 and 0000 1101, respectively. The bitwise operators allowed by the Python language are listed in the following table, along with an example for each. As operands, we utilize the two variables (a and b) mentioned above.

Logical operators in Python

The Python programming language supports the following logical operators. Assuming that variable a contains 10 and variable b contains 20,

Membership Operators in Python

The membership operators in Python check if a sequence of elements, such as strings, lists, or tuples, is present. As described below, there are two membership operators.

Modules

A Python file having a.py suffix that can be imported into another Python program is known as a module.

The module name is changed to the name of the Python file.

1) Class definitions and implementation are included in the module. 2) Variables; and 3) Internally-useable functions.

Working with modules makes the code reusable, which is an advantage of modules.

Simplicity: Rather of concentrating on the full issue, the module concentrates on a tiny aspect of it.

Scope: To prevent identifier clashes, a distinct namespace is specified by a module.

Establishing a Module

making a module with a single function

This software creates a function called "Module" and saves it in a file with the name Yashi.py (the file name plus the.py suffix).

creating a module with a variety of functionalities
We have developed four functions for addition, multiplication, subtraction, and division in this application.

naming the document Operations.py

Functions
A function is a section of code that only executes when called.You may provide parameters—data—to a function.

As a result, a function may return data.

Different Functions

1. User-defined Functions: User-defined functions are ones that we develop ourselves to carry out a certain activity.

As you can see in the Yashi.py file example above, we constructed our own function to carry out certain operations.

User-defined function benefits

User-defined functions make it easier to comprehend, maintain, and debug programs by breaking them up into manageable chunks.
if a program has repetitive code. These programs may be put in a function that can be called to run when necessary.

Give an explanation of the phrase "object-oriented programming."

The object-oriented programming (OOP) paradigm for computer programming organizes software's design on data or objects rather than around functions and logic. A data field with specific traits and behavior is called an object.

With OOP, the focus is more on the objects that programmers want to manipulate than on the logic required to do so. Applications that are complex, large, and often updated or maintained are a suitable match for this style of development. This includes both design and production software as well as mobile applications. For example, system simulation software may be created using OOP.

The strategy is beneficial in collaborative development when projects are divided into groups because of how an object-oriented software is structured. The benefits of efficiency, scalability, and reusing code are also provided by OOP.

What does Python file management entail?

In addition to Create, Open, Append, Read, and Write, Python also supports...

In programming, dealing with files is a regular task. Python's built-in methods for generating, opening, and closing files make managing files easier. While a file is open, Python also enables a variety of file actions, such as reading, writing, or appending data.

How does Python handle file operations?

- Use Python's open() method to open a file
- 'r': This mode indicates that the file is only going to be available for reading.

- The mode 'w' indicates that the file will only be open for writing. ...
- The output of that program will be appended to the previous output of that file, as indicated by the mode 'a'.

What are debugging and error handling?

Therefore, error management is a means to stop a potentially devastating mistake from stopping a program. Instead, your application may notify the user in a far more user-friendly way if an issue does occur, and you can still maintain control over the program.

What do you mean by managing errors?

Error Handling in Compiler Design

Each problem must be found, reported to the user, and then a recovery plan must be developed and put into action to deal with the issue. The program's processing speed shouldn't be sluggish during this whole procedure. Error detection is a function of an error handler.

What are APIs and libraries?

A library is a collection of applications that perform related activities collectively or the same work as a group. Simply said, a library looks like a large piece of code. An API is the interface you use to interact with another system, which may be a library. An API often appears as a group of methods and characteristics.

What is involved in utilizing APIs?

But we're really glad you asked! APIs are an essential component of our digital world and enable billions of digital experiences every minute of every day. The acronym API stands for "Application Programming Interface." APIs are a kind of software interface that let two applications communicate with one another.

Python Data Analysis

Data analysis is the process of gathering, processing, and organizing data in order to make predictions about the future and well-informed data-driven choices.

Finding potential answers to business problems is also helpful. Data analysis is broken down into six phases. As follows:

Request or Specify Data Needs

Data preparation or collection, cleaning, processing, analysis, sharing, reporting

- Which seven phases include data analysis?
- To correctly evaluate data, adhere to following steps:
- Decide on a goal. Establish the main goals and purpose of your data analysis first.
- Choose the appropriate data analytics type to utilize.
- Establish a strategy for gathering the data.

- Gather the data, and then clean it up.
- Analyze the information.
- Visualize the information.
- Descriptive research.

How can Python be used to access SQL?

Using the ODBC Driver for SQL Server, one may connect to SQL Server from Python.

First, connect. pock nan = pyodbc.connect import('DRIVER=Dearth ODBC Driver for SQL Server'; Server: My Server; Database: My Database; Port: My Port; User ID: My Ushered; Password: My Password')

Step two is to insert a row.

Third step: run the query.

How does Python access a MySQL database?

Python connection to a MySQL database

Install the connection module for MySQL. Python's MySQL connection may be installed using the pip command.

Install the MySQL connection module.

Make use of the connect() technique.

Make use of the cursor() function.

Make use of the execute() function.

Using fetchall(), get result...

Close the connection and cursor objects.

Does Python have a place in web development?

Python enables web designers to build websites using a variety of different programming paradigms. For instance, it is appropriate for both functional programming (FP) and object-oriented programming (OOP). Our article on FP versus OOP will explain the distinctions between the two.

Python is a beautiful language. The rules are short and easy, and learning them is entertaining. Although it is a popular choice for beginners, Python is also powerful enough to handle some of the most well-known products and applications in the world from companies like NASA, Google, IBM, Cisco, Microsoft, and Industrial Light & Magic, among others.

Python excels in a number of fields, including web development. Among the many frameworks offered in Python are Bottle.py, Flask, CherryPy, Pyramid, Django, and web2py. These frameworks are used by some of the most popular sites in the world, including Yelp, Mozilla, Reddit, Washington Post, and Sportily. This section's lessons and articles go through Python Web application development approaches with a focus on how to produce workable solutions to problems that ordinary people really need assistance with.

Advantages of Python

- Python is straightforward for new people to use and to learn. This high-level programming language has a syntax that is comparable to English. These factors make the language easy to pick up and adapt to. Compared to Java and C, Python needs less lines of code to achieve the same result. Python's concepts can be applied more rapidly than those of other languages since it is easier to learn.

- Enhanced output: The language Python is quite effective. Developers can concentrate on resolving Python's issues because to its simplicity. More work is done since users don't have to spend hours studying the syntax and functionality of the programming language.

- Flexibility: Users may try new things since this language is so versatile. Users are able to create several new kinds of apps using the Python programming language. The language does not prevent the user from trying unique things. Python is more often used in certain contexts than other programming languages because it provides more freedom and flexibility.

- Large library: When using Python, the user has access to a huge library. The extensive Python standard library has practically all the functions one might possibly need. This is due to the strong support from the local community and corporate funding. Users who use Python do not use outside libraries.

- Community support: Because the Python programming language was created many years ago, it has a well-established community that can help developers of all skill levels, from beginners to specialists. Developers may learn the Python programming language more quickly and completely because to the language's extensive manuals, tutorials, and documentation. Python has expanded more swiftly than other languages because of its supportive community.

The drawbacks of Python

We've already seen several reasons why Python is a wise option for your project. But if you decide to go that route, you need also be mindful of the outcomes.

- Now let's look at Python's limitations in comparison to other languages.

- Speed restrictions
- Python code is run line by line, as we have seen. But since Python is an interpreted language, its performance is often sluggish.

- However, unless speed is a key component of the project, this is not a concern.

- 2. Lackluster Browsers and Mobile Computing
- Python makes a great server-side language, but it's far less common on the client-side.

- In addition, it is seldom ever utilized to build apps for smartphones. The Carbonnelle app is one such example.

- Despite Brython's presence, it is less well-known since it lacks sufficient security.

- Design Limitations

- As you are aware, Python uses dynamic typing. As a result, you are not need to define the type of a variable as you write the code.

- It types with a duck. However, what's that? Simply said, it implies that everything that resembles a duck must be one.

- While this makes coding easier for the programmers, run-time mistakes may result.

- 4. Insufficient Database Access Layers
- Python's database access layers are a little immature in comparison to more popular technologies like JDBC (Java

DataBase Connectivity) and ODBC (Open DataBase Connectivity).

- As a result, it is used less often in large businesses.

- 5. Basic
- No, we aren't joking. The simplicity of Python may in fact be a drawback. Consider what I did. Python interests me more than Java does